ADA TWIST, SCIENTIST

THE WHY FILES

EXPLORING FLIGHT!

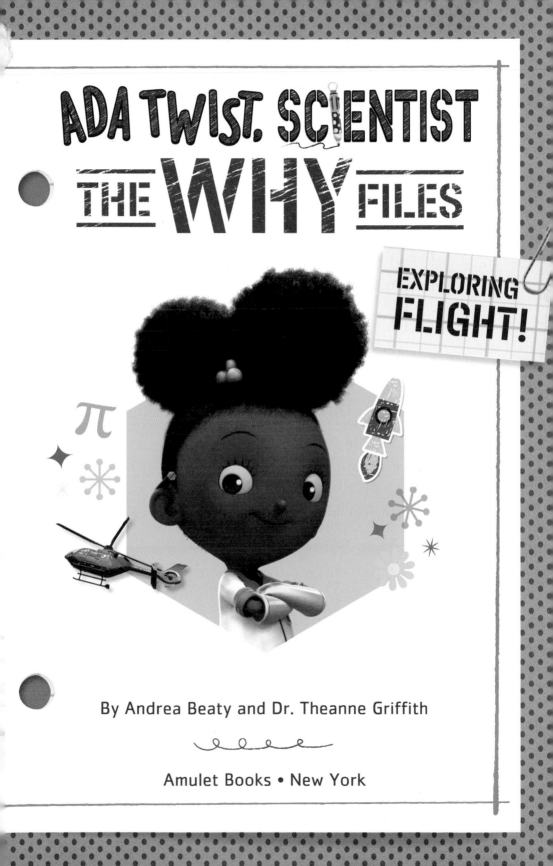

By Andrea Beaty and Dr. Theanne Griffith

Amulet Books • New York

To Ezra. Welcome to the world. —A.B.

For you, Dad. I know you love planes. —T.G.

Library of Congress Control Number 2021912510

ISBN 978-1-4197-5925-3

ADA TWIST ™ Netflix. Used with permission.

Story and text © Andrea Beaty
ADA TWIST series imagery © Netflix, Inc. and used with permission from Netflix.
Book design by Charice Silverman
Illustrations by Steph Stilwell

Amulet Books are available at special discounts when purchased in quantity for premiums and promotions as well as fundraising or educational use. Special editions can also be created to specification. For details, contact specialsales@abramsbooks.com or the address below.

Amulet Books® is a registered trademark of Harry N. Abrams, Inc.

The following photographs sourced from Shutterstock.com. Cover: *hummingbird*, photomatz; *kite*, Photo Melon; *helicopter*: mezzotint; *background texture*: Wasan Srisawat. **Throughout:** *paperclips and sticky notes*, Green Leaf. **Page 2:** Aui Meesri. **Page 3 (top):** Maryna Pleshkun; **(bottom):** SergeyIT. **Page 4:** photomatz. **Page 5:** Photo Melon. **Pages 10, 14, 15:** Lovely Bird. **Page 13:** Potapov Alexander. **Page 15:** J. Borris/Mauritius Images. **Page 18:** JenJ Payless2. **Page 20:** Eric Isselee. **Page 25:** Skycolors. **Page 27:** Plam Petrov. **Pages 28, 29 (bottom):** Sergey Novikov. **Page 33:** Alones. **Page 34:** photowind. **Page 35:** Vera Larina. **Page 40:** Fauzan Maududdin. **Page 41:** Richard Cook. **Page 42:** Marco Tulio. **Page 45:** ohenze. **Page 46:** Doglikehorse. **Page 51 (top):** Petr Simon. **Page 52:** Photos SS. **Pages 53 (bottom), 68 (bottom), 77, 79:** Green Leaf. **Page 55:** mezzotint. **Page 60:** Jimmy Lu. **Page 61:** Ciprian Stremtan. **Page 62:** elitravo. **Page 64:** wewi-photography. **Page 65:** Fexel. **Page 69:** Roman Khomlyak.

ABRAMS The Art of Books
195 Broadway, New York, NY 10007
abramsbooks.com

It's a perfect day! The sky is blue and clear.

If I look up, can I see outer space? **NO!**

I have an observation!

I see planes! Birds! Bees!
Rockets! SPIDERS!!!!

WHAT!?!

HOW DO ALL THESE
THINGS FLY?

It's a mystery! A riddle!
A puzzle! A quest!

Time to find out what flight
is about!

Flight is when an object moves without touching anything on Earth. When something flies through the air, it is called **aviation**. When it flies through outer space, it is called **spaceflight**.

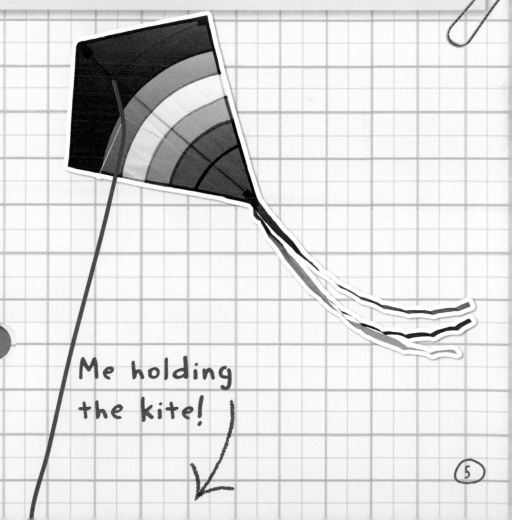

Me holding the kite!

An object needs force to fly. A **force** is a push or a pull that changes an object's speed, shape, or direction. Flight has four forces.

The FOUR FORCES of FLIGHT

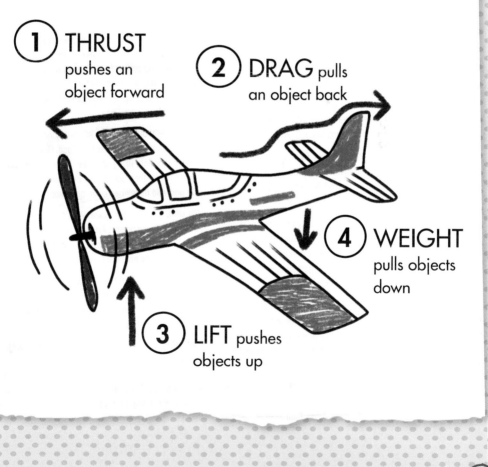

(1) THRUST
pushes an
object forward

(2) DRAG pulls
an object back

(3) LIFT pushes
objects up

(4) WEIGHT
pulls objects
down

When we swing, it can feel like we are flying. A friend pushes us, and we are **thrust** forward as we **lift** up into the air. Our **weight** pulls us down and we are **dragged** backward.

Today, a big bird landed
next to me. I looked at it.
It looked at me.

The bird flapped its wings.
I flapped my arms. One of us
flew away.

Hint: It was not me!

WHY CAN'T I FLY LIKE A BIRD?

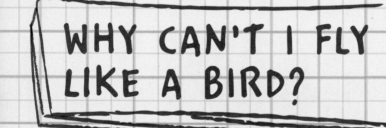

Look! A Bird!
(A poem by Ada Twist)

As I looked up at the big
blue sky,
I saw a bird flapping by.
Now I have questions!
I want to know why.
How do they do that?
And why can't I?

AIR

Birds fly using thrust, lift, weight, and drag! The wings of flying birds are curved on top and flatter on the bottom. This shape is called an **airfoil**.

It makes air move faster over the top of the wing than below. This creates lift that pushes the bird up. A bird makes thrust by flapping its wings. This pushes the bird forward.

thrust →

lift

In flight, the force of lift is stronger than the weight of gravity pulling the bird down. Birds also use their wings to make drag and stop flying. When a bird raises its wings, air moving around its wings slows down. So does the bird!

THAT'S A DRAG!

CAN ALL BIRDS FLY?

Penguins have flat wings that can't make lift. Their wings work like flippers. They can swim!

WE NEED A BRAINSTORM

What could make a penguin fly?

1. Wear a hat with a propeller.

2. I could make parrot wings for them to **flap, flap, flap!**

3. Buy a ticket on South Pole Airlines.

Kiwis are birds that live in New Zealand. They can't fly. Their wings are too small and not the right shape. They walk!

Kiwis are also a green fruit with seeds inside. They can't fly either.

Planes are big. They do not build nests. They do not tweet or have feathers.

Planes do not even flap their wings.

HOW DO THEY FLY?

TWEEEEET!

Plane wings are shaped like bird wings! But how do they make thrust to go forward? Do planes flap their wings? No!

Planes and their wings are made of metal. The metal body of a plane has more weight than a bird. Planes use big engines to make thrust. The plane must go very fast for its wings to make lift. Then the plane can take off!

Cars have engines that move them forward, too. But cars do not have wings. They stay on the ground.

CAR OF THE FUTURE

BIRD SEED

(aka FUEL)

Like birds, planes use their wings to make drag to slow down. When a plane needs to land, it lowers its wing flaps. These flaps change the way air moves around the wings, and the plane slows down. Smooth landing!

You can feel drag, too! When you skate with your hands out to each side, wind moves around them. When your palms face the ground, wind moves around your arms. Not much drag.

What about when you turn your palms forward? Can you feel that? More drag! This way, it is harder for the wind to move around your hands. It slows you down.

Air

LESS DRAG

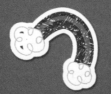

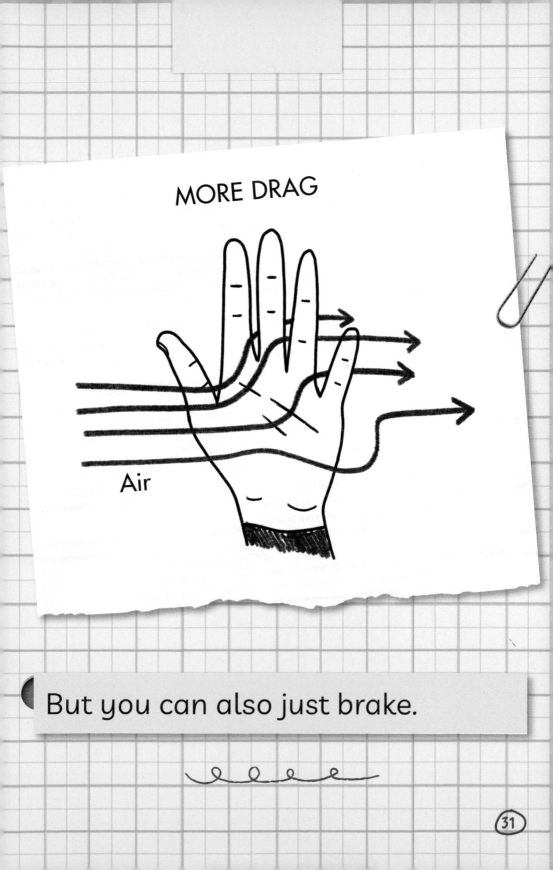

But you can also just brake.

Outer space is far away.

To get there, I need a rocket.

HOW DO ROCKETS FLY?

Rockets are heavy like planes and need big engines and a lot of fuel.

When the engines turn on and the fuel starts to burn up, gas comes out. The gas makes enough thrust to push the rocket into space. Lift off!

If a cat toots, will it scoot? If it toots a lot, will it fly to the moon?

TOOOOOOO

Nope! Even a big, loud fart would not thrust a cat off the ground. No lift. It would just stink!

How do rockets land? For a long time, they did not. They fell all the way from space! The sea is full of old rockets. That is not good for the planet. Plus, it makes space travel cost a lot. So scientists are thinking of cool ways to land rockets. Then they can use them over and over!

A splashdown

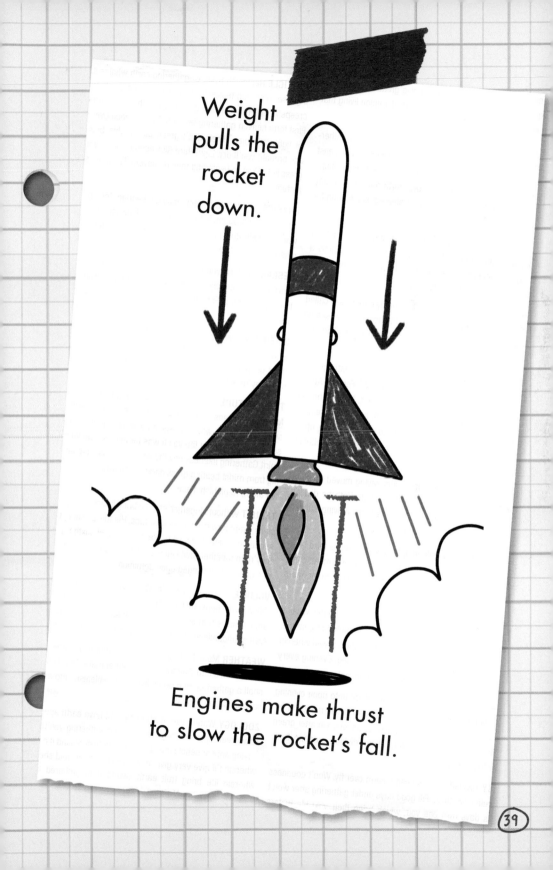

Weight pulls the rocket down.

Engines make thrust to slow the rocket's fall.

Bees are so loud! Buzz!
Buzz! Buzz!

They are big and round. They
have small wings.

HOW DO THEY FLY?

This was a mystery for a long time! For many years, scientists did not think bees should be able to fly. How could something with a big body and small wings fly? How did bees create enough lift? Especially while carrying all that pollen? And how can they stay in the air while flying so slowly?

Bees do not flap their wings up and down like birds. Bees move their wings back and forth. They also rotate their wings. This helps them fly slowly without drag pulling them back.

Bzzz. Hi Bob!

Bzzz.

But wings are not the only thing bees use to fly! They use muscles that make their body twist and turn as they beat their wings. Together, this makes a lot of lift. More than scientists and mathematicians realized! When a bee flaps its wings, air starts to spin below. Faster and faster! Like mini tornados!

AIR

AIR

Fascinating!

A real
tornado!

Over a hundred years ago, people were figuring out how to fly. But not everyone was allowed to learn. Black people and women were not given the same opportunities to fly as others. But these amazing pilots did not let that stop them!

Katherine Johnson

BESSIE COLEMAN was the first Black woman and first Native American woman to get a pilot's license in 1921. She was American, but she had to travel to France to get her license. At that time in the United States, women were not allowed to become pilots. It was even harder for Black women.

In 1935, **WILLA BROWN** became the first Black woman to earn a pilot's license in the United States.

PATRICE WASHINGTON was born in the Bahamas and became the first woman pilot of Bahamasair in 1984. In 1988, she became the first Black woman pilot to work for UPS.

In 1992, **MAE JEMISON** became the first Black woman to go to space. During the STS-47 mission, Mae served as a science mission specialist. She was in charge of forty-four science experiments during the eight days the crew was in space.

Mae Jemison

Bees' wing movements and muscles let them fly backward, too. What else can fly backward?

Planes? No.

Rockets? No.

Birds? Mostly no.

99 percent of birds can only fly forward. But hummingbirds are different. They can twist and turn their wings like bees, so they can fly in all directions. Forward! Backward! Up! Down!

What else can fly in all directions?

A helicopter! A helicopter uses thin spinning blades to fly. Just like a plane's wings, helicopter blades are airfoils. They are curved on top and flat on the bottom. These blades form a rotor. When the rotors spin, they create force. It is a twist! And it is called **torque** (sounds like *fork* but with a *T*).

A REAL-LIFE pilot!

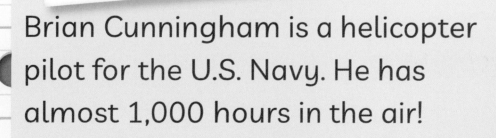

Brian Cunningham is a helicopter pilot for the U.S. Navy. He has almost 1,000 hours in the air!

Wow! That is a LOT of hours!

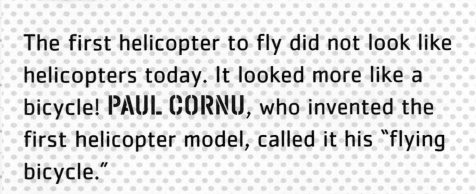

The first helicopter to fly did not look like helicopters today. It looked more like a bicycle! **PAUL CORNU**, who invented the first helicopter model, called it his "flying bicycle."

Women first flew helicopters during World War II. But it was not until 1979 that **MARCELLA HAYES NG** became the first Black woman helicopter pilot of the United States Army. Some people were not happy about that. They took away her right to fly just one year later. Sadly, she never flew a helicopter again.

But that did not stop others from trying to become helicopter pilots. **ANGELA WILLIAMS** was the first Black woman to fly an Apache helicopter in 2000. In 2003, **VERNICE ARMOUR** became the first Black woman pilot in the Marine Corps. She flew the Super Cobra helicopter.

Modern helicopters are about a hundred years old. But almost two thousand years ago, model helicopters flew through the sky in China! They were made of bamboo.

Bees and birds use muscles
for power.
Planes, helicopters, and
rockets use engines.

Kites do not have muscles
OR engines.

Iggy made a shark kite!

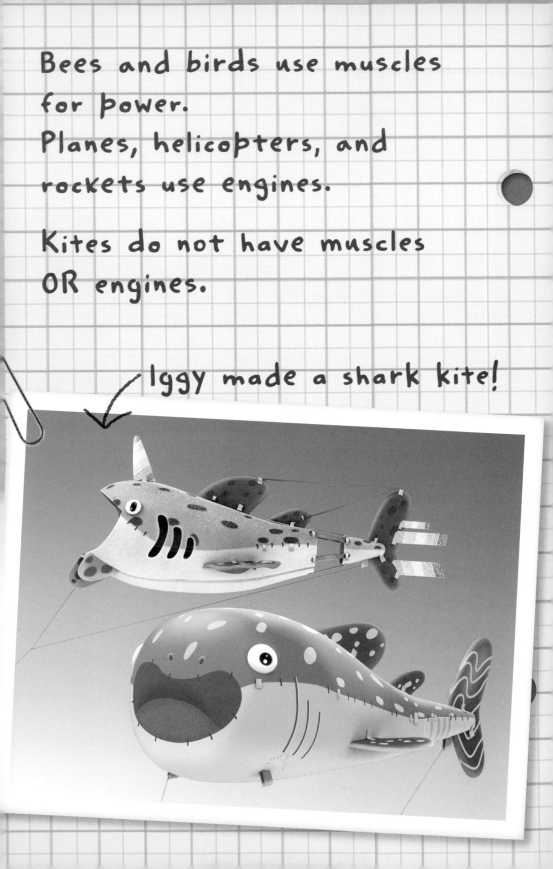

HOW DO THEY FLY?

Kites use the four forces of flight!

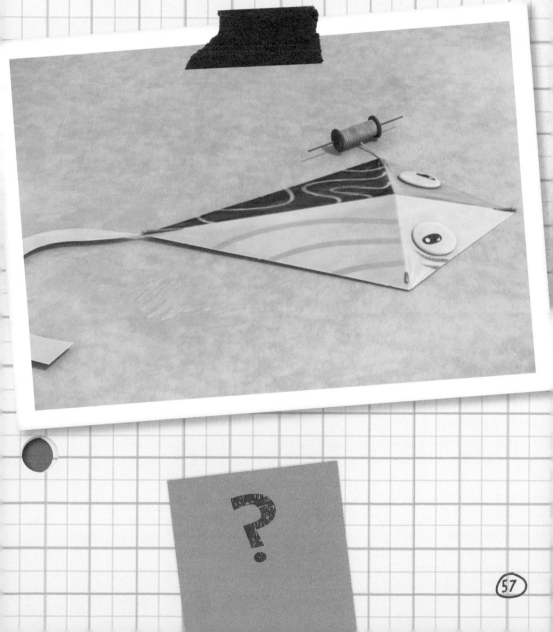

Kites are shaped like plane wings. Air moves faster over the top to make lift. What about thrust? The wind gives them thrust. If the wind stops, they will be dragged down to the ground. Kites are light, but they still have weight!

The kite was invented in Asia, and early models made in China were made with bamboo. Bamboo is light but strong. There is also a lot of bamboo in China. That made it the perfect material for building kites.

Hot-air balloons go up, up, up without wind!

HOW DO THEY DO THAT?

The air inside of a hot-air balloon is heated with a burner. The hot air begins to rise and pulls the balloon up with it. When it is time to land, the pilot opens a vent and allows the hot air to escape.

THE WHY FILES

FIRSTS

In 1783, **PILÂTRE DE ROZIER** and **MARQUIS D'ARLANDES** were the first people to fly in hot-air balloon.

A year later in 1784, **ÉLISABETH THIBLE** became the first woman to fly in a hot-air balloon.

Over 230 years later, **CAPTAIN JOYCE BECKWITH** of Kenya became the first Black woman from Africa to become a hot-air balloon pilot. Her passengers call her Captain Smiles.

A spider just flew by!
I did not see
that coming.

Spiders do not have wings or engines or rockets.

They are not shaped like kites or filled with gas like balloons.

WHAT IS GOING ON?

Spiders can't fly like birds or planes. But they can move through the air! Spiders use silk to spin webs, and they also use it to travel. It is called **ballooning**. On a nice warm day, you can see a spider stick its butt in the air and . . .

The spider sends silk into the air where it forms a triangle-shaped parachute. The wind sends the spider on its way.

The spider's silk catches the air.

What's up? Me!

Warm air rises.

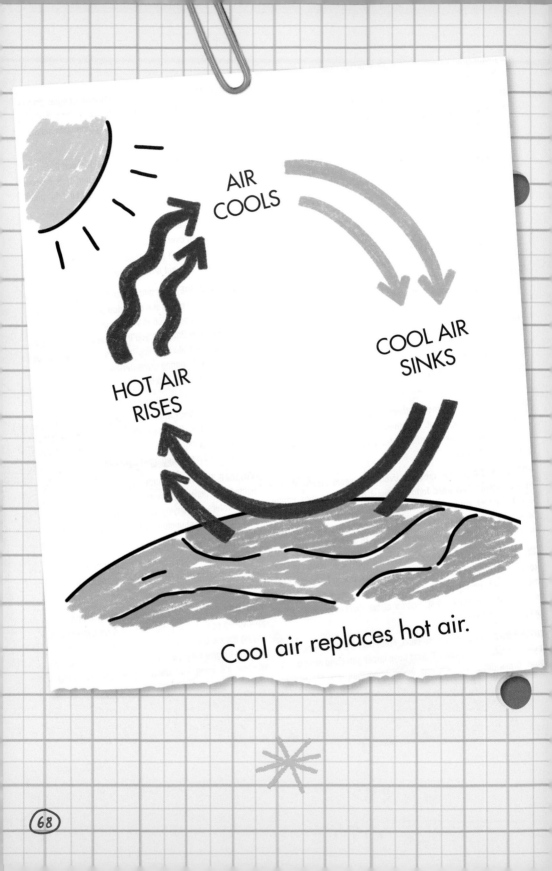

Why do spiders wait for warm days to balloon? Spiders use wind for thrust and lift. Like kites! Warm air is lighter than cool air and rises higher. Lighter air means spiders can travel more easily. There is less weight pulling them down.

Spiders fly like kites!

I have MORE QUESTIONS now than I did before.

Why does each question lead to three questions more?

Is answering that what science is for?

MY QUESTIONS!

What else flies in the air?

Will cars fly in the future?

Why don't penguins wear swimsuits?

Can penguins talk under water?

Do kiwis like kiwi fruit?

Does kiwi fruit like kiwis?

Do spiders wave at each other in the air?

SIMPLE SCIENCE EXPERIMENTS

You can ask a grown-up for help!

AIR AND AIRFOILS

How does fast-moving air make lift?

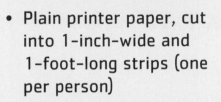

MATERIALS

- Plain printer paper, cut into 1-inch-wide and 1-foot-long strips (one per person)

- Notebook for recording observations

INSTRUCTIONS

1 Hold the strip of paper up to your lips.

2 Blow!

What happened to the paper? Which direction did it move? Why? Write down your ideas

You might guess that blowing on top of a piece of paper will push it down. But it doesn't! It **lifts** it up! This is because of the fast-moving air on top of the paper. Fast-moving air creates less force, or pressure. By blowing on top of the paper strip, there is less pressure on top than underneath the paper strip. This is what causes it to rise! Just like a plane and bird wings!

WE CAN TEST THIS AGAIN WITH ANOTHER EXPERIMENT!

THE PAPER TENT

MATERIALS

- One small piece of paper (3 inches by 4 inches will work)
- One straw
- Notebook for recording observations

INSTRUCTIONS

1 Fold the paper in half. This is your paper tent.

2 Place the tent on something smooth and flat. It could be a desk, table, or even the floor!

3 Rest the bottom of the straw a couple inches away from the opening of the tent.

4 Blow! But not too hard.

5 Write down your observations.

What happened to the tent? Why did it close? The same reason the strip of paper lifted! The fast-moving air going through the tent caused there to be less pressure inside. The force of the air outside the tent was greater than the force of air inside. And just like that, the tent closes!

Can you make your own experiment to show how airflow and airfoils work? Share them using #whyfileswonders.

Andrea Beaty is

the bestselling author of the Questioneers series and many other books. She has a degree in biology and computer science. Andrea lives outside Chicago where she writes books for kids and plants flowers for birds, bees, and bugs. Learn more about her books at AndreaBeaty.com.

Sirk Productions

Theanne Griffith, PhD,

is a brain scientist by day and a storyteller by night. She is the lead investigator of a neuroscience laboratory at the University of California–Davis and author of the science adventure series *The Magnificent Makers*. She lives in Northern California with her family. Learn more about her STEM-themed books at TheanneGriffith.com.

Chris Lo Bue Photography